Vichy France: The History of Nazi Germany's Occupation of France during World War II

By Charles River Editors

Personal Flag of Philippe Pétain, Chief of State of Vichy France (Chef de l'État Français)

D1414567

About Charles River Editors

Charles River Editors provides superior editing and original writing services across the digital publishing industry, with the expertise to create digital content for publishers across a vast range of subject matter. In addition to providing original digital content for third party publishers, we also republish civilization's greatest literary works, bringing them to new generations of readers via ebooks.

Sign up here to receive updates about free books as we publish them, and visit Our Kindle Author Page to browse today's free promotions and our most recently published Kindle titles.

Introduction

Hitler in Paris with the Eiffel Tower in the Background

Vichy France

Emerging from France's catastrophic 1940 defeat like a bedraggled and rather sinister phoenix, the French State – better known to history as "Vichy France" or the "Vichy Regime" after its spa-town capital – stands in history as a unique and bizarre creation of German Fuhrer Adolf Hitler's European conquests. A patchwork of paradoxes and contradictions, the Vichy Regime maintained a quasi-independent French nation for some time after the Third Reich invasion until the Germans decided to include it in their occupation zone.

Headed by a French war hero of World War I, Marshal Philippe Petain, and his later Prime Minister Pierre Laval, Vichy France displayed strong right-wing, conservative, and authoritarian tendencies. Nevertheless, it never lapsed fully into fascism until the Germans arrived to reduce its role to little more than a mask over their own dominion.

Petain carried out several major initiatives in an effort to counteract the alleged "decadence" of modern life and to restore the strength and "virtues" of the French "race." Accordingly, he received willing support from more conservative elements of society, even some factions within the Catholic Church. Following Case Anton – the takeover of the unoccupied area by the Germans – native French fascist elements also emerged.

While the French later disowned the Vichy government with considerable vehemence, evidence such as fairly broad-based popular support prior to Case Anton suggests a somewhat different story. The Petain government expressed one facet of French culture and thought. Its conservative, imperialistic nature did not represent the widespread love of "liberty, fraternity, and equality" also deeply ingrained in French thinking, but neither did it constitute a complete divergence from a national history that produced such famous authoritarians as Louis XIV and Napoleon Bonaparte.

Vichy France: The History of Nazi Germany's Occupation of France during World War II looks at France after its downfall and the occupation that lasted until late 1944. Along with pictures of important people, places, and events, you will learn about Vichy France like never before, in no time at all.

Vichy France: The History of Nazi Germany's Occupation of France during World War II

About Charles River Editors

Introduction

Chapter 1: The Genesis of Vichy France

Vichy France emerged from the unusual circumstances surrounding France's defeat by German in the late spring and early summer of 1940. When Germany invaded Poland in 1939 and conquered the nation in the first example of "Blitzkrieg," the United Kingdom and France declared war on Germany in support of their Polish ally. Though the Soviet Union also invaded Poland on September 17th, 1939, the western Allies chose not to declare war on the second dictatorship, fearing its size and power.

On May 10th, 1940, the Third Reich's Wehrmacht attacked France as well. Bypassing the formidable and effective Maginot Line – which, despite its later reputation, actually functioned effectively in areas where the Axis engaged it – the Germans feinted into Belgium to draw off the British and French armies stationed in northern France, then struck their main blow through the Ardennes Forest.

Heinz Guderian

The Allies believed the Ardennes impenetrable to heavy armor, but Heinz Guderian's and Erwin Rommel's panzers readily traversed the woodland and punched violently westward on a lightning campaign to the Atlantic coast. French soldiers fought bravely and sometimes effectively at specific locations, but multiple factors doomed their efforts overall. Soon, the French Army found itself collapsing and in full retreat.

The Germans themselves expressed astonishment at their degree of success, as Karl von Stackelberg, the war diarist of General Georg-Hans Reinhardt's XXXXI Panzer Corps recorded shortly after crossing the French border:

> It was inexplicable. How was it possible, that after this first major battle on French territory, after this victory on the Meuse, this gigantic consequence should follow? How was it possible, these French soldiers with their officers, so completely downcast, so completely demoralized, would allow themselves to go more or less voluntarily into imprisonment? (Horne, 2007, 271).

France suffered defeat mainly due to its slow, methodical, extremely rigid combat technique, which removed almost all initiative and flexibility from small tactical units actually engaged with the enemy. Against this parched and lumbering orthodoxy the Germans set a dynamic new method of warfare that exploited the mobility advantages of armored attack groups assisted by deadly close air support to the full. The Wehrmacht combined bold, sweeping strategic movements and deep penetration and encirclement with great tactical flexibility created by allowing junior officers maximum independence.

Staggering losses in World War I also made the French leadership reluctant to fight to the last bullet. After losing much of an entire generation of young men in the Flanders bloodbath, and suffering immense damage to their industrial heartland, French demographics and economics remained weak in 1940. Pacifism blossomed, ironically, in the right wing of French politics, as the author Roger Martin du Gard expressed in 1936:

> "Anything rather than war! Anything!... even Fascism in Spain... even Fascism in France: Nothing, no trial, no servitude can be compared to war: Anything, Hitler rather than war!" He was not alone. In the same year, the Provencal novelist Jean Giono wrote: "For my part, I prefer being a living German to being a dead Frenchman" (Christofferson, 2006, 11-12).

The spirit animating Vichy already existed in France during the 20 years before the regime arose. The French, appalled and hamstrung by their losses in World War I, already accepted defeat and collaboration as preferable to another bloodbath.

Simultaneously, and unselfconsciously, the right wing and conservative elements blamed French lack of fighting spirit on the moral "decadence" and "decay" of modernity and urbanization. Both these themes emerged as foundational concepts of the Vichy regime, demonstrating its actuality as an organic outgrowth of interwar French culture, not an aberration from it.

Not just the soldiery but the politicians and the population joined in the flight before the approaching Germans. This enormous rout of the French, both military and civilian, involving both the nominally powerful and the powerless, formed the milieu in which the Vichy government received its initial form:

> The scale of this extraordinary population movement, christened the Exodus, astonished contemporary observers. One described it as resembling a geological cataclysm. The writer-pilot Antoine Saint-Exupéry wrote that from the air it looked as if some giant had kicked a massive anthill. It has been estimated that between 6 and 10 million people fled their homes. The population of Chartres dropped from 23,000 to 800, Lille from 200,000 to 20,000 (Jackson, 2001, 127).

The French government, itself soon on the retreat, found itself hard-pressed to make any decisions at all. With key individuals missing during the "Exodus" and the remaining cabinet on the move, debate and command crashed to a standstill, with occasional spasms of over-hasty attempts at leadership.

Chapter 2: The Last Days of the Third Republic

Paul Reynaud, the 118th Prime Minister of France, occupied his position only two months before finding himself at the heart of this crisis. A well-meaning man who defied the Nazis and spent much of the war imprisoned at Sachsenhausen Concentration Camp and Itter Castle, Reynaud made several critical appointments with a strong bearing on the immediate future of France, for both good and ill.

Paul Reynaud

Attempting to patch up disintegrating French morale, Reynaud ousted officials perceived as weak and placed more energetic men in their place. Charles de Gaulle, then an aggressive and fearless tank commander who had long advocated modern, Blitzkrieg-style tactics, received a promotion to Brigadier General and an appointment as Undersecretary of War, making him prominent enough to launch his coming political career as leader of the Free French during World War II and France itself postwar.

Charles de Gaulle

Reynaud also appointed the fiercely right-wing Major General Maxime Weygand to the post of Supreme Commander of the French Army, too late to accomplish anything besides further confusion in the deliquescing command structure. He also named Marshal Philippe Petain as the Minister of State on May 18th, 1940, hoping to bolster morale through the old general's undeniable bravery, fame, and charisma. Both Petain and Weygand became linchpins of the emergent Vichy state.

Philippe Petain

On May 25th, a French official proposed an armistice with the Germans, just 15 days after the first panzer rumbled across the frontier. Weygand, meanwhile, managed to stiffen resistance briefly and delay the Germans for several days with a defense in depth along several major axes of advance. Nevertheless, the French government abandoned Paris on June 10th, proclaiming it an "open city" as they did so to spare it devastation.

Maxime Weygand

The British Expeditionary Force's evacuation from Dunkirk in late May and early June enabled England to fight on, but enraged both Weygand and Petain against the United Kingdom, inclining both strongly towards making an accommodation with Germany. The government moved to Tours, and there, on June 12th, General Weygand again proposed an armistice with the Germans. Other suggestions included shifting the remains of the French Army and government to the colonial holdings in North Africa, maintaining independence there and using that as a springboard for an eventual return if the British (and possibly the Americans) ever managed a continental offensive.

At this point, with France on the verge of total collapse, Winston Churchill, the Prime Minister of the United Kingdom, attempted to shore up the continental nation with a remarkable suggestion too often forgotten in history books. He suggested a Franco-British Union on June 16th, 1940, which would unite the two countries into one. The French and British Parliaments would merge, all citizens would enjoy one common citizenship, and the French and English army leadership would form a War Cabinet having equal control over a unified military.

Sir Orme Sargent put the case for this astonishing proposition forcefully:

such a system of close and permanent cooperation between France and Great   Britain – political, military, and economic – as will for all practical purposes make   of the two countries a single unit […] Such a unit would constitute an effective   counterweight to 80 million Germans in the middle of Europe (Shlaim, 1974, 31).

Churchill's suggestion, though well-received by many of the French, failed to carry the day in part because Reynaud, embarrassed by the confusion of his cabinet, neglected to invite the charismatic man to the meeting where his government discussed that very matter. Without Churchill's forceful personality, and with many of the French officials believing his absence "treachery" (rather than ignorance of the meeting thanks to Reynaud's error), support for the Franco-British Union waned.

Winston Churchill

When the Germans took Paris on June 14th, Reynaud's government retreated from Tours to Bordeaux. Reynaud attempted to gain an assurance of assistance from American President Franklin D. Roosevelt, though the eventual response naturally proved negative in the face of the American public's pacifism. In the meantime, Weygand refused any course except armistice, wanting to preserve French military honor.

At this critical juncture, Deputy Premier Camille Chautemps made the fateful suggestion that the French government find out what terms the Germans offered for an armistice, without actually negotiating with them. This gave the "armistice faction" of Petain and Weygand 13 members out of the 19 forming Reynaud's cabinet.

The British actually prepared a Declaration of Union uniting the two countries, approved by Charles de Gaulle, then serving as Reynaud's representative in London. When telephoned with the news, Reynaud reacted ecstatically: "Union with Britain […] meant independence for us at exactly the time when we had only the choice between union and certain slavery under the German jackboot" (Shlaim, 1974, 51).

However, when he presented the idea to the Council of Ministers, only a few supported the offer, with the majority loudly proclaiming their preference for the Nazis over the British, including Marshal Petain.

Reynaud, shocked and astonished at their attitude, remarked "those who rose in indignation at the idea of union with our ally were the same individuals who were getting ready to bow and scrape to Hitler" (Shlaim, 1974, 53). Petain, Weygand, and most of the other men apparently preferred the German jackboot. Deeply saddened and despairing, Reynaud resigned as Prime Minister late on the 16th. This automatically led to Petain, as Minister of State, rising to become head of the French government.

The other French leaders underestimated Petain, believing him senile at age 83. Instead, the Marshal showed remarkable vigor, acumen, and slyness, along with a robust physique for a man of his age. Though he played a quiet role in the days before his ascension to the head of the French government, this largely represented a pose over a canny and keenly ambitious mind seizing the chance to pounce on the reins of power.

Chapter 3: The Armistice and the Birth of Vichy

Events in France continued unfolding rapidly. On June 17th, Petain announced the armistice before its actual signing, leading many to believe it a *fait accompli*. On the 18th, Hitler informed Mussolini that he would receive very little French territory – essentially only a few small towns near the border his men seized during the fighting. For the most part, Mussolini's untrained and ill-equipped soldiers bloodied themselves valiantly but uselessly against the Alpine Maginot Line, while their Duce heaped scorn on them for a situation objectively due entirely to his poor decisions.

Petain Meeting Hitler

General Charles Leon Huntziger, later commander in chief of Vichy ground forces and who died in an airplane accident in 1941, met with Adolf Hitler himself on June 22nd, 1940 to negotiate the actual terms of the armistice. The negotiations, of course, consisted of the Germans dictating terms and the French accepting them.

To further underline their dominance, the Germans chose the Compiegne Wagon as the scene for the ceremony. This railway car, used as an office by French Marshal Ferdinand Foch in World War I, served as the venue for Germany's signing of the armistice ending the first global conflict in 1918. Huntziger now signed the armistice acknowledging French defeat in the same carriage, at the town of Rethondes. The Waffen SS demolished the Compiegne Wagon, then a trophy in Crawinkel, Germany, in March 1945 using explosives, thus preventing its recapture by the Allies.

Hitler soon left the negotiations in the hands of Generaloberst Wilhelm Keitel. The terms of the 24-article armistice proved comprehensive. The Germans designated an Occupation Zone encompassing approximate 60% of France's land area, including the country's industrial north, Paris, and the entire Atlantic seaboard down to the Spanish border. The Unoccupied Zone – soon to be the French State or "Vichy France" – included the remaining 40% of the nation in the southeast, except for a few slivers of territory granted to Mussolini.

Wilhelm Keitel

Other terms included the creation of a small, impotent "Army of the Armistice," the automatic remanding of political refugees in Vichy territory to German custody, and the holding of 1.5 million French POWs in Germany as slave labor and hostages. The Third Reich threw the French a few crumbs, such as the retention of their fleet in their own Mediterranean ports and continued ownership of their overseas colonies. The Germans insisted that the French disarm their fleet and disband most of its personnel, however.

Huntziger initially rejected these terms and engineers from both sides rigged a telephone line permitting a direct conversation between Keitel and Weygand. Weygand also attempted to soften the terms, but met with a stony rebuff from Keitel. The Germans held all the trump cards and the French must acquiesce or suffer total subjugation.

Weygand only agreed to leave 1.5 million POWs in German hands because he believed that England would fall within 3 weeks, ending the war and freeing the prisoners. The Armistice also made Vichy France liable for the (then unspecified) costs of paying for the German occupation forces in the Occupied Zone. The Germans left to the French the option to determine the exact form of government, location of the French State's capital, and other details of government and social organization in the "Free Zone." Faced with an ultimatum, Weygand authorized Huntziger to sign at 6:50 PM on June 23rd.

The American journalist William Shirer, present in the Wagon during the negotiations, took down a personal statement by Huntziger after the signing. The defeated French general, his voice quaking with emotion, said:

> I declare that the French Government has ordered me to sign these terms of armistice… Forced by the fate of arms to cease the struggle in which we were engaged on the side of the Allies, France sees imposed on her very hard conditions. France has the right to expect in the future negotiations that Germany show a spirit which will permit the two great neighboring countries to live and work in peace (Shirer, 2011, 728).

The signing of the Armistice effectively founded Vichy France. Hitler's purpose in allowing this quasi-independent protectorate appeared to be dividing France to ensure its weakness, while shifting much of the administrative burden and cost of government onto the French themselves.

Crucially, it also prompted the French to retain their fleet, which, while denied to the Germans, also remained firmly outside British control. Without some equivalent of Vichy France, the French Navy would likely defect to England, greatly strengthening the vessel strength of the already formidable Royal Navy. For the moment, the German dictator enjoyed a scheme permitting him to eat his cake and have it, too.

Just as the Treaty of Versailles at the end of World War I forced Germany to muster only a very small standing army with practically no modern vehicle support, so the Army of the Armistice became a pale shadow of the huge forces deployed by France prior to June 22nd, 1940. The Germans limited total size to 100,000 enlisted men and officers, including an Army of 84,000, a combined Navy and Air Force of 10,000, and "Guards" totaling 6,000. The French organized these forces into two army groups, each consisting of four divisions (Sumner, 1998, 37-38).

The Germans disallowed anti-tank weapons in French hands. The Armistice Army used MAS36 rifles, Hotchkiss machine guns, 50mm grenade launchers, 81mm mortars, and 75mm field guns as its main weaponry. Besides soft-skinned vehicles, the Armistice Army fielded Panhard AMD armored cars armed with an extra machine gun in place of the original anti-tank gun. The Army also included dragoon and cuirassier cavalry.

Additionally, the Germans allowed the French to keep tens of thousands of troops (and, in the case of North Africa, over 100,000) active in their overseas colonies and imperial holdings. The Third Reich even permitted expansion of these forces after they fought and defeated Free French soldiers on several occasions. These armies also retained a few hundred Renault R35 and Somua S35 tanks, plus AT-gun armed armored cars.

The Armistice Army itself served mainly to keep internal peace and order, preventing armed insurrection and later dealing with the armed Resistance. Many men chafed under the German yoke but considered it their duty to remain at their posts until relieved or until Vichy fell entirely and ceased to be a viable state. Vichy overseas military units, on the other hand, often served as combat soldiers in World War II actions.

Chapter 4: Britain Attacks the Vichy Fleet

The fate of France's naval assets, now that many of them resided in the custody of the Vichy Regime, exercised the statesmen of Britain, the United States, Nazi Germany, and the French State more than any other issue relating to occupied France during 1940. Vichy needed to keep the fleet out of British hands to avoid vengeful annihilation at the hands of the Wehrmacht, but also prevent the Germans from appropriating it. The Germans wanted the French ships but found Vichy too useful in other ways to openly seize them and drive Petain's government into the arms of the Allies. Britain desired the ships for its own fleet, but also wished to keep them out of German hands at any price.

Simultaneously, the Vichy government found itself in another delicate situation. It could stave off German efforts to involve it in direct action against the British if it defended its colonies strongly. Keeping the colonies put their resources at Vichy's and the Third Reich's disposal, while denying those resources to the Allies. Each intact colony also provided a potential base of operations if the far-flung, global conflict shifted to its region.

However, the French State wanted to avoid direct action against the English as much as possible. Prodding the British lion might awaken the beast to fury and a full-scale attack on Vichy's overseas possessions. Petain's military policy needed to remain forceful and aggressive enough to keep the colonies, but circumspect enough to prevent total war between the United Kingdom and the French State. Complicating the situation, the Vichy administration contained both "hawks" – like Maxime Weygand and Pierre Laval – and "doves," many of them influential over different policy areas.

Pierre Laval (left) with Carl Oberg, Head of German Police in France

The British seized all French naval ships at anchor in English ports before dawn on July 3rd, 1940. Most seizures proved bloodless, but a scuffle ensued on board the French destroyer *Mistral* in Plymouth harbor. Even worse followed on the submarine *Surcouf* in Devonport. 30 British submarine sailors and a detachment of 30 Royal Marines boarded the *Surcouf* at 4:30 AM, led by Commander Dennis Sprague. These men carried revolvers, rifles with fixed bayonets, and language cards with four French phrases written on them, including the command "Up with your hands!"

The French officers and men on board the *Surcouf* had resolved on tragic defiance. As soon as the first French sailor on watch spotted English soldiers clambering onto the submarine's deck, he ran below, and the French closed and locked all four hatches from within. Officers and selected men began destroying code books and vital pieces of equipment chosen days before in case of just such an eventuality.

British Lieutenant Francis Talbot, an experienced submarine officer, soon discovered that the hatch in the conning tower featured catches that could be opened from the outside for purposes of rescue, exactly like an English submarine. The British levered the hatch open and swarmed aboard, rousing the crew and collecting the officers.

The French admiral on board the submarine left to speak indignantly to the British authorities, leaving Corvette Captain Louis Jacques Henri Pichevin in command. Pichevin, irked by the fact that most of the equipment slated for destruction remained intact, surreptitiously sent an electrician to cut the lights, giving the French the opportunity to finish destroying their technology and code books. Lieutenant Talbot spotted the man leaving and sent a petty officer after him. When the electrician switched off the lights, the petty officer battered him into submission with a large wooden mallet (carried for forcing hatches) and turned the lights back on almost immediately.

Sprague, enraged, ordered Pichevin and his officers off the *Surcouf*; the French refused point-blank, and Sprague called for backup. As a few armed British sailors pushed into the room, a gunnery officer named Pierre Bouillaut drew his .32 ACP MAB Model D pistol and opened fire, as he himself later recounted:

I took a pace forward and shot at Commander Sprague, Lieutenant Griffiths, the two English sailors, and then again at their officers. As I was shooting I moved to   the companionway – that was the moment I was wounded – and I fired at a sailor   who, no doubt kneeling in the Command Post and showing only his steel helmet at   the top of the companionway, was shooting at me (Smith, 2010, 33).

Bouillaut mortally wounded both Sprague and Lieutenant Patrick Griffiths. One of the .32 bullets chopped through a large vein in Sprague's shoulder, causing him to bleed profusely. Griffiths, on the other hand, suffered a wound in the liver. The men bled for 25 minutes before receiving first aid in the confusion, and 45 minutes passed before a doctor reached them. Both died in the hospital approximately 24 hours later.

As Bouillaut opened fire, the submarine's doctor, Robert le Nistour, dashed for his cabin to retrieve his .25 caliber pistol to join the fight. Leading Seaman Albert Webb, standing with a fixed bayonet beside Sprague, apparently mistook him for the shooter and ran after him, bursting into the cabin.

A luckless engineer named Yves Daniel sat inside, destroying blueprints and other papers. Le Nistour fired all seven rounds in his pistol into Webb's body at point blank range, first wounding, then killing him. Webb fired one shot, wounding Daniel in the shoulder. The momentum of his rush carried him the last few feet, however, and his dead weight drove the bayonet into Daniel's chest, slipping between the ribs to pierce his heart and kill him almost instantly.

Chief Petty Officer John Mott shot Bouillaut with his heavy .45 caliber revolver, wounding the Frenchman. Realizing the hopelessness of their situation, Pichevin disarmed Bouillaut – who seemed ready to go on fighting – and called up to the English above that they wanted to surrender. Talbot allowed this provided they came up one at a time so the British could search each for weapons.

The brief fight for the *Surcouf,* named for the Napoleonic era privateer Robert Surcouf, ended. No retribution fell on the Frenchmen involved, in part due to Britain's squeamishness over seizing the ships of a recent ally. In fact, the English sent even Bouillaut, the instigator of the fray, home to France in mid-December.

Compared to the colossal struggle unfolding across the world, the bloody shootout in the French submarine occurred on a tiny scale. However, it represented the first time since 1815 that British and French military personnel fought each other, and was the first combat in the following low-key war between Britain and Vichy France.

The English also decided to eliminate as many French ships in Mediterranean ports as they could in order to weaken a possible Axis navy incorporating them. On the same day as the gunfight on *Surcouf,* July 3rd, Force H of the Royal Navy under Vice Admiral Sir James Fownes Somerville sailed to take control of the French ships at Mers el-Kebir in French Algeria near Oran – or, in case the French refused to surrender or scuttle them, to attack and sink them.

Despite deep misgivings and a self-confessed feeling of shame, Vice Admiral Somerville led his ships to within striking distance of the anchored French vessels. Somerville's superior, Admiral Andrew Cunningham (Commander-in-Chief, Mediterranean Fleet) shared the Vice Admiral's aversion to attacking the French. He wired London:

"Am most strongly opposed to forcible seizure of ships […] nor can I see what   benefit is to be derived from it" (Grainger, 2013, 43).

Winston Churchill remained adamant and the mission went ahead.

The British force, including the aircraft carrier *HMS Ark Royal,* the battleships *Valiant* and *Resolution,* the battlecruiser *HMS Hood,* a pair of cruisers, and 11 destroyers, attempted to hem Admiral Marcel-Bruno Gensoul's ships in the harbor, taking such steps as mining several of the main channels. Meanwhile, Somerville sent a French-speaking captain, Cedric Holland, on the destroyer *HMS Foxhound* to negotiate.

Gensoul procrastinated as long as possible to give his ships time to ready for combat, and eventually Somerville gave the order to attack. The *Bretagne* exploded, killing around 900 men, and the *Dunkerque* suffered 210 KIA, while sustaining enough damage to force its pilots to run it aground to avoid sinking. In all, 1,297 Frenchmen died at a cost of 2 British deaths. However, the *Strasbourg* and several destroyers eluded the British in a display of virtuosic seamanship, joining the main Vichy fleet at Toulon.

Admiral Gensoul got the "last word" on the engagement the following day when he oversaw the burial ceremony for the French sailors killed at Mers el-Kebir and declared: "If there is a stain on the flag today, it is certainly not on yours."

Chapter 5: Operation Menace – Dakar

Following Mers el-Kebir, the Free French under Charles de Gaulle and the French State under Petain vied for control of France's numerous African colonies during the late summer and autumn of 1940. Following a visit to Brazzaville in the Congo by de Gaulle, French Equatorial Africa, or AEF (Afrique Equatoriale Francaise), switched allegiance to the Free French and the Allies. This included the territories of French Cameroon, the French Congo, Chad, Gabon, and Oubangui-Chari.

While gaining these territories represented a feather in the cap of the Free French leader, several of the most valuable possessions remained aligned with Vichy France. These included French Algeria and French West Africa, an extensive region encompassing Niger, Senegal, Mauritania, the Ivory Coast, French Guinea, Upper Volta (Burkina Faso), Dahomey (Benin), and French Sudan (Mali). The capital and major port of Dakar represented the main prize of the region from the belligerents' standpoint.

The plan to take Dakar, Operation Menace, involved sending a contingent of British ships under Admiral John H.D. Cunningham (a different man from the Admiral Andrew Cunningham involved in Mers el-Kebir) to the port in September. The ships carried a force of Free French soldiers and General de Gaulle himself.

With rather blithe optimism, Churchill – who rammed the plan through over the objections of practically every naval minister and officer involved – believed the Vichy French garrison of Dakar would immediately switch sides when offered the chance to do so by no less a personage than de Gaulle. In the event the Vichy men resisted, the Free French could storm ashore supported by the guns and aircraft of the British flotilla. This fleet included the much-traveled aircraft carrier *HMS Ark Royal,* the battleships *Barham* and *Resolution,* five cruisers, 10 destroyers, and 8,000 Free French troops on transports.

Prior to the expedition, the Free French in Britain proved extraordinarily incautious about keeping it a secret, as planned. Practically every dinner involving French officers witnessed these men shouting "A Dakar!" as a toast, with Gallic panache and total disregard for discretion. Additionally, several large bundles of propaganda leaflets aimed at the Dakar garrison broke open in port in a high wind, and thousands fluttered away through the streets long before their slated time of distribution.

The fleet sailed on September 1st, 1940 and reached Dakar on September 23rd, with heavy tropical fog lying densely over the ocean. The first news the Vichy garrison received of their uninvited guests came when two light aircraft from *Ark Royal* landed at the Ouakam Fighter Base to try to persuade its personnel to switch sides. Instead, the air crews took the seven men on board prisoner. In an astonishing display of military incompetence, the Free French pilots carried a list of all 14 secret Gaullists in Dakar, which the Vichy governor, , used to carry out immediate arrests.

Fairey Swordfish torpedo bombers flew low over Dakar and dropped tens of thousands of leaflets, which served no purpose except to alert the garrison of the task force's existence and proximity. The Vichy battleship *Richelieu,* licking its wounds in the harbor, drove off the Swordfish with a vicious hail of anti-aircraft fire.

A band of Free French sent to the Dakar quay in a launch barely escaped capture, and the shore batteries opened fire on the British ships, which returned fire, though the aim of both parties suffered due to the fog. De Gaulle spoke by radio to Governor Pierre Boisson and received defiance in return.

In the first exchange of gunfire, a shell from one of the shore batteries pierced the hull of the cruiser *HMS Cumberland,* killing seven men and causing enough internal damage to force the ship to sail away. The British soon got revenge when the cruiser *HMS Dragon* destroyed the Vichy submarine *Persee* using depth charges, though most of the crew escaped alive.

Late in the afternoon, both sides made additional moves, their intentions screened from the other party by the thick, persistent fog. De Gaulle's French marines attempted to land at Rufisque Bay, 13 miles from Dakar, but a galling fire from Vichy Senegalese troops on the beach caused their motor launches to turn back.

At the same time, a number of Vichy ships sallied from Dakar harbor to attack the unseen enemy visible only as occasional glimpses of superstructures or hulls and the glow of gun discharges in the fog. A destroyer, *La Malin,* and two cruisers, *Montcalm* and *Georges Leygues,* sailed directly past the British without making contact. However, the well-named destroyer *L'Audacieux* ("The Audacious") steamed directly towards the Australian-crewed ship *Australia.*

Captain Robert Ross Stewart quickly canvassed his officers and crew for French-speakers. Since most came from "Down Under," far from Europe, almost none did. However, Royal Navy Midshipman Stuart Farquharson-Roberts, just 18 years old, did:

'I called down, "I know some French, sir." He told me to come and give him the   words for: "If you don't turn back I'll sink you." This I did with the aid of a   dictionary for "sink."' They flashed this over with an Aldis lamp and L'Audacieux   made a one-word reply [...] J-A-M-A-I-S. "'They say "Never," sir," I translated. –   "Are you sure?" – "Yes, sir." –

"Right, open fire'" (Smith, 2010, 73).

Pounding *L'Audacieux* with shells, *Australia* killed 81 men on board the ship and set it afire. Abandoned by its crew, the destroyer eventually drifted ashore and beached. Nevertheless, the Vichy defenders baffled the British and Free French at every turn. Early the following morning, Governor Boisson telegraphed the message "France has entrusted me Dakar. I shall defend Dakar to the end" (Smith, 2010, 76) to the French State.

The British made futile bombing runs on the 24th, and their vessels shelled Dakar but failed to silence its batteries. Finally, on the 25th, the Vichy French took the initiative again. The submarine *Beveziers*, commanded by Corvette Captain Pierre Lancelot, lurked near the battleships *Resolution* and *Barham*. Waiting until the British ships started to come about – necessarily slowing as they did so and presenting easier targets – Lancelot ordered his sub to surface and his men to fire four torpedoes.

Three of the four missed, but the fourth struck *HMS Resolution* squarely, killing one man but also flooding a boiler room and part of the interior. This not only greatly reduced the ship's mobility but created a dangerous list to port. The destroyer *HMS Foresight* attempted to destroy *Beveziers* with depth charges, but the French submarine slipped away unscathed. The crippling of a battleship during a relatively unimportant mission (from the British point of view) prompted London to break off Operation Menace immediately, making the Dakar attack a Vichy victory.

Captain Evelyn Waugh, unpopular officer of the Royal Marines and later author, wrote in a letter composed as the flotilla limped away that he overheard the British seamen singing a newly improvised song commenting on the uselessness of the failed mission, with a chorus running:

"We went to Dakar with General de Gaulle.

We sailed round in circles and did bugger all" (Smith, 2010, 81).

The Vichy French Air Force in North Africa launched retaliatory bombing raids against the British base at Gibraltar in response to the attack on Dakar. Raids by 50 and 100 bombers respectively on September 24th and 25th proved quite inaccurate, typical for the time, killing only a few civilians and sinking a British armed trawler, *HMT Stella Sirius*.

One serious consequence of the disastrously bungled effort, besides the loss of life and damage to several capital ships, involved Britain's loss of faith in de Gaulle, a sentiment rapidly transmitted to the United States government:

The British decided that the Free French could not be trusted with intelligence information. [...] for the rest of the war, de Gaulle was kept in ignorance of every operation involving France. Dakar also reinforced the argument of those in the   British government who wanted to build bridges to Vichy instead of backing a   maverick general – 'that ass de Gaulle' as Cadogan wrote – who seemed to have   little support among the French (Jackson, 2001, 366).

In fact, the Free French, despite their undeniable indiscretion in England, betrayed nothing to the Vichy government. Dakar failed, not because the Vichy French received forewarning from their feckless compatriots in exile, but because the commanders on the scene used their resources better than the British or de Gaulle, acted with less restraint, and had men whose fighting spirit remained largely untouched by the collapse of French Army morale in the home country in May to June 1940.

Chapter 6: Further Operations

De Gaulle's Free French rebounded from their defeat at Dakar and won several notable successes in the following period. In early November, de Gaulle's men took Libreville in Gabon, seizing the portions of French Equatorial Africa remaining in Vichy hands.

The next summer, in July 1941, Operation Exporter occurred, with a large-scale battle between Allied and Vichy forces in the Syria-Lebanon Campaign. 34,000 Free French, Australian, British, and exiled Czechoslovakian troops fought 45,000 Vichy French soldiers and 90 tanks under the leadership of General Henri Dentz. The campaign lasted slightly over a month and ended in Allied victory, with 4,500 Allied casualties against 6,000 to 8,000 Vichy killed and wounded and 5,500 more defectors.

The final major action involving Vichy French forces occurred with the Battle of Madagascar between May 5th and November 6th, 1942. General Armond Leon Annet commanded the Vichy soldiers, during a protracted campaign in which more men on each side died of tropical diseases than of enemy action.

One strange addition to the Madagascar action came from the presence of two Imperial Japanese Navy (IJN) midget submarines in the coastal waters, supporting the Vichy French. Indeed, much of the reason for invading Madagascar consisted of denying it to the Japanese, who, in 1942, eyed it as a possible naval and air base for attacks even farther west. The British sank both, however, and the French eventually surrendered, putting paid to both Vichy and Japanese ambitions in the region.

Chapter 7: Vichy France's Culture and Government

Though the Germans offered to let the French State government use Paris as their capital (alongside the German military government of the Occupation Zone), the surviving French vassal state's leaders preferred a location on their own territory. For a very brief interval, Petain headquartered his government at Clermont-Ferrand. However, on July 1st, 1940, the Marshal moved the capital to Vichy.

A city of spas and casinos, Vichy possessed two qualities making it peculiarly suited to serving as capital for the remains of the French nation. In the first place, the numerous large, sturdily made, and quite elegant hotels converted readily into government buildings, as did some of the larger casinos. In the wake of France's fall, the government experienced very little competition from tourists for use of these facilities, rendering their takeover smooth and effective. The pleasant and picturesque conditions in and around the city, and the numerous amenities and sources of entertainment, likely sweetened the choice also.

Secondly, Vichy boasted a superb telephone system, recently modernized and representing one of the finest and best-maintained in France. The obvious advantages of such a reliable, powerful telecommunications system to a government coordinating the administration of a new country and keeping close watch on the Third Reich's intentions provided the rest of the impetus for the selection.

Just nine days after the move to Vichy, on July 10th, the National Assembly of Vichy France convened in the Grand Casino, the structure with an interior space big enough to seat all 569 delegates. Their first vote, whether to make Petain head of state, worked overwhelmingly in the Marshal's favor. 471 delegates voted for him, 80 against, and 18 abstained. This vote suspended Parliament until further notice and made Petain Head of State. It also enabled creation of a new Vichy constitution.

The Papal Nuncio, echoing Rome's loathing of democracy, declared the result a "miracle." In fact, fear of the Germans and the oily political maneuvering of the ultra-right wing politician Pierre Laval ensured the outcome. Petain made Laval Deputy Prime Minister as a reward for services rendered, though he hated the man personally.

The newly elected Head of State set about reshaping France into the state he believed it should be. Replacing the slogan of "Liberty, Equality, Fraternity" with "Work, Family, Fatherland," Petain began his program of National Revolution immediately, though most classified its tenets as reactionary rather than revolutionary:

> He told the French that they had lost the "spirit of sacrifice," which had been replaced by a decadent "spirit of pleasure." It was now time for "atonement for their sins." [...] Immediately "Papa" Pétain shepherded his children into [...] an idealised

attempt to re-create old France – Catholic, agrarian, authoritarian, with an emphasis on order and obedience (Callil, 2006, 162).

While Petain had no objections whatsoever to concentrating most constitutional powers in himself, he rapidly headed off the idea of a national party similar to Germany's Nazi Party or the Communist Party in Soviet Russia. Many outright French fascists left for Paris in disgust when they realized this, preferring the company of the Germans to Petain's pragmatic authoritarianism. Petain, for his part, viewed them as a threat to his power and made no effort to retain them in Vichy.

After a fashion, Petain reigned like a modern version of a medieval king. While a Council of Ministers met weekly, most decisions occurred in small private meetings between a handful of ministers and the Head of State. Petain made and broke ministers frequently, while relying on a handful of men he liked, trusted, or otherwise deemed useful. Etiquette and protocol became extremely important.

Petain showed favor by allowing people to dine with him or ride in his car (which, of course, also gave them the opportunity to explain their ideas and try to win legal and financial support for them), and displayed his disfavor by keeping other individuals at arm's length. Petain also included many military officers in his government, with Weygand forming one of the "standbys" who persisted through the Head of State's frequent reshuffling of men and departments.

The Vichy State even adopted its own flag – the red, white, and blue tricolor, but modified with the addition of a double-headed ax to the center white field. Rendered in red, white, and blue also, this ax represented the throwing ax of the Frankish warriors of the Dark Ages, the "francisca," or "Francisque" in Vichy terminology. The design deliberately mimicked the "fasces" emblem of the Italian fascists.

As Petain consolidated his hold on Vichy France in a haphazard but determined manner, Pierre Laval played his own game. Displaying the clashing traits of fascism and pacifism, Laval frequently visited Paris to confer with the Germans, and, in late autumn of 1940, persuaded Petain to meet with Adolf Hitler and begin the program of "collaboration."

Adolf Hitler and Philippe Petain met on October 24th, 1940 at Montoire, a meeting arranged and pushed through to actuality by the Deputy Prime Minister, Pierre Laval, who loathed Britain, strongly favored Germany, and wished to fully embrace Hitler's fascism. Each leader attempted to manipulate the other in order to gain something that he wanted, and neither succeeded, though Hitler felt the results represented a fairly positive outcome. The Fuhrer opened the exchange, after the initial handshake between the two leaders, with a direct attempt to enlist Vichy France in the planned attack on England:

> I regret, Marshal, to be meeting you in such circumstances. I know that you did not want this war that was declared by a French government taking orders from England. [...] France has been defeated, and I am certain to soon defeat England as well [...] She relies on the United States and Russia in vain (Corvaja, 2008, 139).

Petain, far too wily to be drawn into a situation where the Germans used the French as sacrificial shock troops in future combat with the British, also proved adroit enough not to offer the German dictator an outright refusal. The Marshal used several tricks familiar to those dealing politely with an unpleasant interlocutor in all places and eras. He claimed difficulty in understanding Hitler's statements due to hearing problems. Then, he told Hitler his government would "study" the matter with great interest, a courteous verbal dodge for indefinite postponement without bald rejection.

Once the Fuhrer exhausted his arguments, Petain took his turn to try and extract concessions from the Third Reich's hegemon. The head of Vichy flatly listed a number of details of the Armistice he saw as problematic and wanted rectified as soon as possible:

Since we are talking about peace and collaboration between our two countries, it would be interesting to know what destiny Germany has in mind for France. This would be a very good time to measure German good will. There are some very urgent questions to be discussed: the release of over two million French prisoners of war; a more humane set of regulations... (Corvaja, 2008, 139-140).

Hitler waffled, saying he would look into the problems once England fell. The conversation provides an intriguing snapshot of the relationship between the German dictator and the Chief of the French State. Each man clearly felt dissatisfaction with the arrangement and wanted more concessions.

Hitler desired enthusiastic – and martial – support for Third Reich aggression, while Petain wanted a somewhat more equal partnership rather than a strict master and vassal arrangement, expressed through easing of the harsher terms imposed on France. Neither leader yielded to the other's immediate demands and instead chose to avoid a breach by promising to do something undefined at an unspecified point in the future.

The British and Free French feared Hitler and Petain signed a secret compact at their meeting, but in fact, neither put their signature to any documents. The Fuhrer indicated he would address all of Petain's concerns if the French collaborated willingly. Believing this promise – or at least hoping it might prove true – the Marshal, attempting to retrieve all French POWs prior to the winter holidays in 1940, made a speech later to associate him forever with treason and collaboration.

The continued survival of an independent Britain represented both a curse and a blessing to Vichy. On the one hand, it meant Hitler's prisoners of war remained interned in Germany. On the other, it provided Vichy with some leverage against excessive Third Reich demands. As long as England remained in the fight, the Vichy government could threaten to transfer their ships to Royal Navy control in order to keep Hitler's demands slightly in check.

Laval, now assistant prime minister, continued his machinations and independent action following the Montoire meeting he orchestrated. Fanatically anti-British and pro-German, Laval's high-handedness infuriated many in the Vichy government, including Petain himself. As Laval continued ahead with all the subtlety of a bulldozer, pursuing an ever-more Hitler-centered policy, he set forces in motion too strong for him to resist.

While many ministers desired Laval's downfall, the Interior Minister Marcel Peyrouton took action. He readied his paramilitary Brigade Mobile for action in case the ousting of Laval prompted civil strife.

The opportunity for Laval's removal came with a bizarre gesture by Adolf Hitler. Wishing to make a conciliatory move towards the French that would cost him essentially nothing, the Fuhrer offered to return the remains of the Duc de Reichstadt, Napoleon's son, from Austria to France. Petain assented eagerly and Laval also gave his blessing to the scheme. The French people, with characteristic pithiness, soon developed the popular phrase "What we want is not bones but meat" (Smith, 2010, 92) to express their concern with food shortages and their indifference to the return of the long-dead imperial heir for burial in Les Invalides.

The men opposed to Laval, fearing the incident would cement the Germanophile's position in the government, cast about for a solution. Francois Darlan, Minister of Marine and the man whose decision to send French shipping to the colonies kept it out of the hands of the Germans, devised a scheme to effect his rival Laval's fall.

Though he did not attempt to prevent the return of the Duc de Reichstadt's ashes, he told Petain that Laval meant to kidnap the aged Marshal during the funeral ceremony and usurp power for himself. Petain believed Darlan – or accepted the excuse to rid himself of the much-loathed Laval – and ordered the Laval dealt with. The Interior Minister Peyrouton urged Petain to have Laval shot. Petain, however, preferred to arrest and detain the Deputy Prime Minister instead.

Pierre Laval's fall came suddenly on December 13th, 1940, at precisely the moment when the heavy-featured, slick-haired fascist thought himself most secure. The men sent to arrest him first cut the telephone wires connecting the Hotel du Parc to Paris so that Laval could not inform the Germans of the event. They also arrested Laval's chauffeur and impounded his car.

Ralph Heinzen of the United Press, serving as American correspondent reporting on Vichy, entered the hotel and told Laval of the situation. Laval refused to believe Heinzen until he opened the door of his suite:

glaring back at him were a bunch of Peyrouton's finest in their distinctive black   leather jerkins and steel helmets and the rare French MAS M38 sub-machine guns   which should have gone to the army. 'What swine! And it's Friday the 13th,' said Laval, slamming the door.

'They're out to get me and I've nothing to defend myself   with' (Smith, 2010, 93).

The internal power struggle attracted the attention of the Germans, and Laval remained in custody only briefly. However, the move vastly increased Petain's popularity in the short run, as many people viewed Laval as a traitor. Petain appointed Pierre-Etienne Flandin to the post of Deputy Prime Minister following Laval's fall, a move that pleased the Americans and British while infuriating the Germans. In fact, Flandin proved as avid a collaborationist as Laval, though he possessed a less obnoxious personality.

Flandin also remained in his new post for only a short period of time. The man who headed the anti-Laval clique, Francois Darlan, supplanted him in February 1941 as a peace gesture towards the Germans. Darlan almost immediately collected huge amounts of power, adding the titles and responsibilities of Minister of Defense, Minister of the Interior, Minister of Foreign Affairs, and successor to Petain to his portfolio.

Francois Darlan

Darlan rejected the Vichy "nation of peasants" vision and attempted to build a modern economy based on technology. He rejected cultural modernism, however, and fully endorsed Petain's patriarchal, authoritarian, and highly conservative social programs. Though personally indifferent to the Jews, he accepted their persecution as the price needed to help keep the Germans from meddling overmuch in Vichy's internal affairs.

Darlan believed that Germany's victory would permit France to remain a relatively major power and retain its colonial empire. The truth of such a viewpoint remains impossible to test. He correctly forecast, however, that a British victory would result in the dismantling of France's empire and the nation's relegation to third-rate global status:

> If we collaborate with Germany… that is to say, if we work for her in our factories
> […] we can save the French nation; reduce to a minimum our territorial losses in the
> colonies and on the mainland; play an honourable – if not important – role in the future
> Europe. My choice is made: it is collaboration… France's interest is to live and to remain
> a great power… […] I see no other solution to protect our interests (Jackson, 2001, 181).

Vichy collaboration, of course, did nothing to avert this outcome, but Darlan committed to it nevertheless in the belief it would. As summer of 1941 arrived, Darlan offered new levels of military cooperation, especially in Africa, while demanding ever more strongly that the Third Reich reciprocate by granting some Vichy France desires. In particular, Darlan wanted the French prisoners still held in Germany in vast numbers returned, and a sharp cut in Germany's devastatingly high occupation costs.

Hitler ignored all efforts to extract more equal treatment for the French State. Darlan made more concessions, removing Weygand in favor of General Alphonse Juin and increasing the harshness of Vichy's rule to match fascist standards more closely. None of this helped. To the Germans, the Vichy French represented no more than vassals, obliged by their defeat to obey, and not partners, or even junior partners.

When the United States entered the war in late December 1941, Darlan alone of all Petain's leading ministers proved perspicacious enough to see the writing on the wall. Understanding that Germany would likely fall before the American juggernaut now that it roused itself to action, Darlan strongly suggested a U.S. alliance in place of collaboration with the Germans. Whatever his many faults, the 122nd Prime Minister of France enjoyed a clear appreciation of the world's actual balance of military power.

Petain failed to share his lieutenant's vision, and Darlan's fall inevitably ensued. The Head of State forced him out of office on April 18th, 1942 and replaced him with Pierre Laval. The hated "Don Pedro," as his opponents called the unpopular politician with his thick, allegedly Spanish-looking mustache, returned triumphantly to power. As a consolation, Petain made Darlan Commander in Chief of Vichy France's army.

Like the Biblical dog returning to its own vomit, Laval immediately renewed his avid dedication to collaboration with the Germans and even strengthened it. Totally disregarding western Europe and America's viable democratic tradition, he cast the struggle as a choice between the victory of Hitler or Communism:

> "I desire the victory of Germany, for without it bolshevism would tomorrow install
>
> itself everywhere" (Christofferson, 2006, 77).

Ignoring the widespread spasm of disgust his naked collaboration prompted in the French, Laval commenced first the "*releve*," a voluntary labor service in which the Germans repatriated one French POW for every three workers who went to Germany to help run the Third Reich's farms, factories, and mines, and then the involuntarily *Service du Travaile Obligatoire* (STO) in early 1943 when the French showed scant enthusiasm for working as semi-slaves of the Germans in facilities regularly subject to Allied bombing.

Even the Germans recognized the deep loathing Laval's actions awakened in the hearts of his countrymen:

> "The enactment of the [STO] compulsory labour law and the anti-Jewish campaign, which is incomprehensible to the French mind... seem to be the major causes of the fall in Laval's prestige" (Christofferson, 2006, 79).

While Laval vigorously completed the work of alienating the Vichy population from the French State's government with his lickspittle collaboration, Darlan had one final, dramatic role to play in the slowly unfolding Axis defeat. In October 1942, his 29-year-old son Alain caught polio during a visit to Algiers in French North Africa. Alain Darlan served a double role, arranging food shipments from the African colonies to the hungry citizens of Vichy France and keeping in contact with the Americans through ambassador Robert Murphy.

On October 9th, 1942, Alain reached Algiers carrying a startling message for Murphy. The elder Darlan suggested an alliance between the Americans and the Vichy military, followed by American landings in Vichy France and a joint campaign to eradicate the Germans from French soil. Alain expressed even more enthusiasm for the idea than his father. However, he found Murphy absent and not due to return until the 11th, and in the meantime, a violent, dangerous case of polio sent him to the hospital in critical condition.

Darlan flew to see his son on October 28th, returned to France on October 30th, then flew back to Algiers on November 4th when it appeared almost certain Alain would die. The younger Darlan eventually rallied, and on November 7th, his father prepared once again to return to Vichy.

Even as Darlan settled down to a celebratory dinner that evening, 700 Anglo-American ships swept towards the coast of French North Africa, preparing to carry out history's then-largest amphibious assault, Operation Torch. When Murphy brought the news to Darlan early in the morning on the 8th, the first botched landings already began. Lieutenant Colonel Edwin T. Svenson led the 634 Minnesotan soldiers of the 3rd Battalion, 135th Infantry Regiment, U.S. 34th Infantry Division ashore near Algiers, but almost at once found himself obliged to surrender. Totally lacking anti-tank weapons, he found his men under attack by Renault R-35 tanks and gave up rather than suffer annihilation.

This unimpressive arrival infuriated Darlan rather than inclining him to join with the Americans and their French figurehead General Henri Giraud. Though the Allies soon put 35,000 men ashore with more to follow, the Vichy French initially fought back and achieved some local successes. In other areas, the spearheading Americans and the follow-up British troops took their objectives and established beachheads for more landings.

Henri Giraud (left) with Charles de Gaulle

Finally, on November 10th, most of the fighting ended and Darlan, as Vichy France's Commander in Chief, ordered all his forces to join the Allies, a command generally followed. This action prompted disastrous political consequences for the Vichy government. Hitler, naturally, viewed this as a complete discrediting of Vichy independence, since the French failed to provide protection to the Mediterranean flank of the Axis. On November 11th, 1942, the Germans launched Case Anton, invading Vichy territory and establishing direct control over the formerly quasi-independent nation.

Darlan made a speech on the radio which suggested to some he wished to supplant de Gaulle as the leader of the Free French:

> Germany's aim is now clear. That is to wipe out France. […] No one of us must any longer hesitate to do his duty which is to crush Germany and Italy and liberate the

country. French Africa is the only place in the world where our flag flies freely, where the army has its weapons, the navy flies it ensign and the air force uses its wings. We are the sole hope of France, let us show ourselves worthy of her (Smith, 2010, 245).

Darlan's triumph remained brief due to an assassin's bullet. A Royalist youth, Bonnier de la Chapelle, mortally wounded Darlan in his office on December 24th with two pistol shots. The French captured him and shot him with unseemly haste at dawn on December 26th, not even permitting him time to finish his Catholic confession in direct contravention of French custom.

The haste of de la Chapelle's execution hints strongly at a motivated attempt to silence him by those who arranged Darlan's death. Darlan represented a minor embarrassment to the Anglo-American Allies, and a slight chance exists they arranged his murder, but given his cooperation and the fact they gained nothing tangible by his death renders this unlikely. Vichy revenge also remains possible but scarcely probable.

General Henri Giraud presents the strongest candidate for the prime mover behind Darlan's assassination. Darlan threatened to replace him as de Gaulle's chief rival for leadership of the Free French. Giraud also later showed himself capable of reckless, unilateral action in defense of his position and in pursuit of additional power. Whatever the case, however, the Vichy government saw its opportunity and fabricated a dying statement from Darlan placing blame for his death squarely on the English.

The Vichy state existed not merely as a ramshackle, quasi-monarchist government but also as a unique cultural and social milieu. Much of Vichy French culture centered around Petain's efforts to recreate a supposed "pure, strong" France with ancient virtues restored and the "decadence" of modernity, personal freedom, and democracy swept away. These efforts echoed those of Germany to reconnect with a mythical "Volk" era.

As part of this effort, Vichy France imposed censorship and frequently issued its own "news" stories supporting a narrative of a hostile, Jew-ridden Britain and a cleanly, forthright Germany representing European renewal. Vichy's enforcers, however, lacked the murderous clout of the Gestapo, and the French press remained restless, almost intransigent at times, despite being badgered into observing the letter of the law.

Alexandre Varenne, the fanatically republican editor of *La Montagne*, published in Clermont-Ferrand, annoyed the censors by continually trying to publish articles containing actual news items and opinion pieces rather than Vichy's clumsily canned propaganda. He also wrote many bold letters directly to Petain, constantly protesting censorship and blasting it as both tyrannical and idiotic:

if the government wishes to be maladroit that is its business. What concerns me is that they dare to use outrageous procedures like this toward French newspapers who make a point of honor of not being subject to anyone: "Publish everything I send   you, in the form that I require, or I will shut you down." Such is the system they are   trying to impose upon us. This is a system of an occupying power, not of a regular   government (Sweets, 1994, 143).

Vichy beliefs coalesced around the youth and intellectual center of a specific school, the Ecole Nationale des Cadres d'Uriage, or, more simply, Uriage. Like similar youth organizations and schools in Nazi Germany and Fascist Italy, Uriage worked to shape the minds of the next generation of French leaders, officers, writers, artists, and similarly prominent people in culture and society at their most formative stage.

The emergent Vichy ideology at Uriage drew on the most reactionary Catholic writers of the later 19th century, and thus won over at least some of the conservative church leaders to lend it support and legitimacy. Even those prominent Catholics who failed to warmly embrace Vichy remained only feebly dedicated to resistance until the Germans effectively took over in 1942, or stayed essentially neutral. Uriage – seeking a "new Middle Ages" – and Vichy thought in general soon acquired a flavor of dogmatic Catholicism.

Though the Uriage school developed and continued the anti-republican, anti-Semitic, pro-totalitarian Catholic youth organizations of prewar France, it also gained support from important Protestant leaders. Rene Gillouin, a prominent French Protestant writer and enthusiast for German fascism, vigorously championed the development of Uriage while writing ultranationalist speeches for Petain on the side.

The Petainists not only promoted Uriage but started various youth movements also, such as *Jeune France.* This offered the double benefit of not merely indoctrinating the next generation of cultural, social, and military leaders with Vichy ideology, but also absorbed active young men who probably would otherwise have found themselves unemployed in the occupied nation's wheezing economy, and thus might have opposed the regime.

The main school soon relocated to the village of Uriage, taking its name from this locale, and occupied the Chateau Bayard, the home castle of France's most famous Renaissance knight. It received funding of 2 million francs and a 50-strong staff of support personnel. The young men wore a blue and black uniform, including a beret and necktie, and followed a regimen involving military, aristocratic, and strongly religious elements.

Father Rene de Naurois, one of Uriage's guiding spirits, spoke contemptuously of the concept of "littleness" (and its attendant benevolent overtones) in French culture:

There are things that condense an entire mentality. The fact, for example, that after the war of 1914-1918, there were French newspapers called... Le Petit Meridional,
Le Petit Journal, Le Petit Dauphinois, Le Petit Parisien,... culminating in the Petit Echo
de la mode. The little Frenchman, his little wife, in his little house... was a whole psychology,

the antithesis to expansion, risktaking (Hellman, 1993, 31).

Uriage attempted to produce an austere, disciplined, active, and obedient elite for diverse roles within the Vichy state. The men trained there acquired a distaste for democracy and personal freedom, a belief in puritanical sexual and social mores, and above all a deep and abiding loathing for communism in any form. The school's program also emphasized team spirit, positivism, and a relentless near-worship of "the fatherland."

Counterbalancing these tendencies, some of Vichy France's important leaders espoused right-wing secularism and pragmatic anti-clericalism. Francois Darlan himself represented this viewpoint, expressing contempt for Uriage's "virgin seminarians" and preferring experienced, cynical men of the world, whom he thought better adapted to dealing with France's problems with Germany and England than ascetic idealists.

While Uriage mostly trained young men for leadership, the Petain government attempted to thrust women back into domesticity. Recognizing the long French feminist tradition, the Vichy Regime threw women a few crumbs, but nevertheless focused strongly on social engineering and the legislation of gender roles:

> The restoration of 'natural' female characteristics became one of the regime's priorities. The fight against depopulation, carried over from the Daladier period, became even more familialist thanks to the influence of Catholics [...] Vichy's draft constitution declared the family to be the basic unit of society. Divorce was restricted (except in the case of mixed marriages involving Jews); women were barred from certain jobs and abortion was made a 'crime against society' (Passmore, 2013, 359).

Defiant and individualistic, the French did not automatically accept these attempts to funnel them into officially determined channels. Many people pushed back, particularly as the Vichy Regime, for all its authoritarianism, initially lacked the systematic organs of state terror that Nazi Germany, Fascist Italy, and Soviet Russia deployed from their earliest days. Of course, following effective occupation by the Germans in late 1942 in response to Operation Torch and Darlan's defection to the Allies, openly fascist ideals came to prevail more and more frequently in Vichy French society, backed up by vicious Gestapo repression and new fascist organizations such as the Milice.

French Milice

Nowhere did Vichy France prove its authoritarian nature more clearly than in the categories of people it chose for persecution. Some of these, such as Nazi spies, would have been treated as enemies by even the most democratic nation. However, Vichy afflicted the Jews with rigor above and beyond anything the Germans initially compelled it to, and sent thousands of dissidents, socialists, communists, and even people who spoke their mind too freely to concentration camps in Algeria or other locations.

Even before later persecutions and roundups of Jews to appease the bloodlust of the Nazis, Vichy's leadership began to sever Jews and others from public life. The Minister of Justice, Raphael Alibert, assisted by a clique of fanatical right-wing Catholic officials and dignitaries, carried out several peaceful purges of the government at all levels.

Alibert began his attack on the Jews almost immediately, depriving 6,000 of them of their French citizenship and rendering them stateless persons in their own homeland. In August 1940, just a month after Petain's takeover of practically all constitutional power, Alibert and his cronies used a law against secret organizations to oust no less than 15,000 Freemasons from public service jobs.

Alibert targeted the Freemasons due to a belief they promoted secularism (Hellman, 1993, 18). In October, the Statut des Juifs ("Statute on the Jews") evicted thousands of Jews from government jobs and laid the groundwork for making their participation in various private professions illegal as well.

From the beginning, Vichy France's economic subservience to Germany stood out starkly. The division of the country itself permitted the Third Reich to skim off the cream of France's modern industry, much of it located in the northern lowlands. Nor did German economic exploitation end there. The "Thousand-Year Reich" squeezed every possible drop of tribute out of the French State on various pretexts, leaving a very austere and straitened lifestyle in its Gallic vassal nation.

Outrageously large German demands on the French State prevented it from ever achieving more than a sort of "modern subsistence" economy. The Germans confiscated most of the rolling stock from France's railways, siphoned off most modern raw materials such as oil, rubber, and steel delivered from the French colonies, and demanded huge cash payments to maintain their occupation forces. The Germans, in fact, set the cost of occupation 50 times higher than the actual price, using the difference to fatten their war chest. The list of other impositions presents startling reading:

> In 1943, Germany was taking 50 per cent of French iron ore, 99 per cent of French cement, 92 per cent of French lorries, and 76 per cent of French locomotives. The Economic Section of the MBF estimated that by the end of 1943 as much as 50 per cent of all French non-agricultural production was for German purposes   (Jackson, 2001, 230).

As part of Petain's efforts to "reform" France and return it to a more pristine and "moral" state, the Marshal's National Revolution supported a strong back to the land movement. Vichy France idealized country living as a source of virtue, health, strength, and fecundity (the last a genuine issue a nation with weak demographics), while excoriating cities as the hotbeds of modern decadence and decay.

To some extent, the Vichy leaders simply made the most of the situation given them. Germany appropriated much of the best modern industry of France and left the French State with less developed, more agricultural areas. Petain "made a virtue of necessity" and attempted to raise morale and national loyalty by depicting the heavy agricultural bias of Vichy territory as a situation suited to France's natural strengths.

A strong ideological undercurrent also flowed through these propaganda efforts, however. Nazi Germany idealized the farmer and the warrior as the two timeless pillars of the "Volk." Vichy's right-wing leaders similarly conceptualized a "nation of peasants" as an ideal, and Petain even created the office of Minister for Peasant Restoration. The Vichy intelligentsia argued that luring

> 'the city dweller back to the open air, this uprooted person often intoxicated by the vitiated atmosphere and sophisms of a totally debilitating milieu, to put him back in immediate contact with the soil, the love of which remains so profoundly anchored to the heart of the peasant, is a work of public health and social pacification' (Pearson, 2008, 18).

This rhetoric initially produced strong support for the Vichy Regime among rural people. Petain held them up as exemplars and, at first, won their loyalty with this flattery. But the bitter, concrete reality of disastrous French State economics soon squandered this goodwill. As inflation mounted, the government attempted to stem it by putting price controls on agricultural products.

Though food, in particular meat, skyrocketed in price, the cost of everything needed to produce it – machinery, tools, buildings, and land – rose even faster. Meat prices increased by 200% by 1942, but production costs shot up 300%, cutting back sharply on supply. The government attempted to drive down the price of pork especially vigorously, and as a result, pork vanished from most markets by 1942.

From brief enthusiasm, the "peasants" and farmers of France transformed swiftly into Petain's bitterest enemies. They willingly assisted Allied airmen escaping from the authorities to seek repatriation via Spain and often helped the Resistance also. As Robert Grasset of the Food Ministry noted in a report:

> "At the present time, the discontent in the agricultural class that has not ceased to grow during the past months has reached a level that those who live outside   agricultural circles cannot imagine." (Sweets, 1994, 79).

The Third Reich demanded much of France's agricultural output for itself, leaving the French with inadequate nutrition. Added to the excessive costs of farming and Vichy's tone-deaf price control policies, this led to rural impoverishment. Food shortages also plagued the French State despite produce brought in from Algeria and other African colonies. During the brief diplomatic flirtation between the Allies and Vichy after the successful defense of Dakar, American food aid helped fill bellies, but from 1942 onward this source of supply also vanished.

By the time of D-Day invasion, years of hunger made the French so lean and bony that German officials, trying to escape by donning civilian clothes, frequently suffered capture in any event because their plump, fleshy appearance marked them out clearly as occupiers. German caloric intake remained mostly above 2,400 calories daily, while statistics compiled by the French and the occupiers themselves highlighted the difference:

Food supplies had been devastated by the war and German requisitioning. In 1945

grain production was one-half of prewar output. Food rationing remained in place well into the postwar period, although caloric intake per capita increased   dramatically from 900 calories per day in 1944 to 1515 by May 1945   (Christofferson, 2006, 199).

The intense shortages of nearly every kind of modern material also led Vichy France to exploit the forest land covering approximately 20% of French territory. At the same time, the French State genuinely espoused a program of reforestation, and of reclaiming maquis (scrubland) for new forests. The urge to reforest France predated Vichy and, indeed, the war years themselves.

The French believed maquis, or Mediterranean scrubland, occurred due to human over-exploitation and that wetter, more productive forest could replace it. Though still debated by environmental scientists to this day, the notion supported reforestation efforts and a bold program of expanding forest reserves.

These positive plans, however, soon foundered under the pressure of German occupation and the dearth of raw materials it caused. The Vichy French, rather unwillingly, turned to the forest and its timber reserves to compensate for other shortfalls. The head of the Forestry Administration, Charles Colomb, noted that France's woodlands underwent notable exploitation because:

almost everyone expects something from [them] that will help them survive these difficult times: householders need fuel for their fireplaces; farmers, litter for their animals; bakers, wood for their ovens; tanners, bark for their leather; transporters, wood or wood charcoal for their gazogènes; and, finally, industrialists [need] raw   materials... for their businesses (Pearson, 2008, 45).

Gazogene vehicles, including both trucks and cars, helped solve the immediate problem of massive fuel shortages. The Germans naturally appropriated all of France's petroleum imports for their own use, since they already experienced difficulties with keeping the Wehrmacht supplied with gas to run its tanks, trucks, and halftracks. A gazogene vehicle mounted metal cylinders on the roof, serving as a furnace to burn charcoal and generate gas to run the vehicle's engine.

Though the Vichy French staved off outright disaster with wood used as a construction material, fuel source, means of winter heating, and so on, extraction of this resource proved difficult and time-consuming. Many timber resources lay far from established major roads and rail lines. Furthermore, due to the hundreds of thousands of young men still in German hands, 35% of Vichy France's trained foresters languished in remote foreign prison camps, greatly reducing the skilled labor force available to harvest the wood and manage the woodland for continued production.

Vichy succeeded in maintaining a minimum level of modern activity by using the forest but, overall, failed in both its reforestation aims and its desire for a "peasant state." The "peasants" found themselves alienated and after the war soon gave place to technologically advanced, well-educated farmers. While Vichy's intentions about reforestation stand as uncharacteristically benign and positive, the harsh reality of German occupation and tribute demands forced exploitation in place of woodland expansion.

Chapter 8: German Occupation and Allied Liberation

The German invasion of Vichy, given the operational codename Case Anton, occurred on November 11th, 1942 in response to Operation Torch and the defection of France's empire to the Allied cause, with Francois Darlan leading the way. Even as German panzers rolled south to take over key strategic positions, a Third Reich emissary named Krug von Nidda arrived at Petain's lodgings to give him a letter personally prepared for him by the Fuhrer, which ran in part:

Monsieur le Marechal, I have the honour, and at the same time the sorrow, to inform you that in order to avoid the danger which threatens us I have, in agreement with the Italian government, been compelled to give the order to my troops to cross France [...] in order to occupy the Mediterranean coast, and [...] to take part in the protection of Corsica against the [...] aggression of Anglo-American armed forces (Smith, 2010, 240).

Hitler cast his invasion and direct takeover as a protective action to shield Vichy France from the western Allies. He fooled nobody, but scarcely needed to. Most of the Vichy soldiery stood down without a murmur and tamely handed over their weaponry to the Germans. They did refuse, however, to part with most of their firearms when the desperate local Resistance asked for this type of material aid.

The final flicker of independent French spirit in Vichy, outside the Resistance, came in Toulon, where most of the Regime's remaining ships lay at anchor. The Germans meant to take these by surprise and hand them over to the Italians. However, they neglected to cut the telephone lines leading from the office of one Vichy admiral after capturing him, and he managed a brief call to the men in charge of Toulon. With desperate speed, the French scuttled their fleet to keep it out of German hands, an act of defiance completed just a few hours before German tanks rolled into the town and halftracks packed with panzergrenadiers followed.

Petain and Laval, the two chief leaders of Vichy, accepted the German dominance over their formerly pseudo-independent domain quietly. Both men retained power, albeit with German oversight, and all the perquisites attending it. The Fuhrer, in fact, expanded Laval's governmental role by allowing him to issue legal decrees on his own initiative, putting him nearly on a par with Petain. Indeed, Laval acknowledged his treason and the hatred the French held him in with remarkable candor:

> When General Weygand informed him that his policy was opposed by 95 percent of
> the French, Laval snorted back that the figure was closer to 98 percent. Although Petain
> protested the German takeover of Vichy, he did so only to appease French public opinion
> (Christofferson, 2006, 79).

Petain, oddly, grew more popular even as French loathing of Vichy reached fresh heights. The Germans and Laval expanded the forced labor demands of the STO, driving thousands of young Frenchmen to join the Maquisards, or rural Resistance.

The ominous Klaus Barbie, an SS man and member of the Gestapo with the sinister patience of a hunting beast while in the field combined with psychopathic rage when torturing prisoners while out of it, installed himself at Lyons and began systematically tracking down Jews and Gaullists for immediate execution or deportation to concentration camps.

Homegrown French fascists also sprang up, as though the German invasion sowed dragon's teeth in Vichy France. The brutal paramilitary Milice under Joseph Darnand climbed from power to power. The organization first came into its own in August 1943, when Darnand swore personal allegiance to Hitler and received an SS rank in return. The Germans gave the Milice weapons and loosed it on France to hunt down their enemies. Darnand gave an outline during a speech of the goals he ascribed to his thugs:

> Against Gaullist dissidence, for French unity, / Against Bolshevism, for   nationalism, /
> Against the leprosy of the Jews, for French purity, / Against pagan Freemasons, for Christian
> civilization (Christofferson, 2006, 81).

The Milice exhibited a very idiosyncratic interpretation of "unity, purity, and civilization." Given the power to convoke their own courts and act as arresting officer, judge, jury, and executioner, they ran amok in France during the remaining period of occupation. They stole what they fancied, raped any woman they found attractive, and engaged in gruesome torture and killing for sport and to terrorize the population.

A Recruitment Poster for the Milice

At the same time, the Milice worked to carry out Hitler's will, fighting the Resistance, suppressing dissent, and ferreting out Jews for immediate extermination or to be sent to the living death of the concentration camps. The organization boasted around 15,000 active members at its height, though many more men joined and then failed to participate, using their membership as a way to avoid forced STO labor service.

Late in 1943, Petain made a last feeble effort to transfer much of the French State's power to the National Assembly. Hitler reacted ruthlessly to this effort to shake off the German and collaborationist yoke, sending SS men to the town of Vichy and threatening to use violence unless Petain yielded. With no force of his own to back up his will, Petain yielded on December 4th to 5th, handing over almost all authority to the pliant Laval and staying as a mere shell and figurehead retained solely for his popularity.

When an Allied bombing raid hit Paris on April 20th, 1944, a month and a half prior to the D-Day landings, Petain went to the city for the first time since assuming control of Vichy. He did so without German approval, and highlighted this fact with a speech made to the adoring crowds who greeted him:

Today, it is a first visit I am making to you. I hope I will soon be able to return to Paris, without being obliged to forewarn my jailers; I will be without them and we will all be at ease (Griffiths, 2011, 249).

As the Allies rolled forward across France in summer of 1944, both Petain and Laval attempted to open negotiations with them on behalf of Vichy. The Germans, however, determined to prevent Petain's defection. Seizing him on September 7th, they drove the 88-year-old Marshal out of his country by limousine to the German town of Sigmaringen, where he remained in comfortable imprisonment for the rest of the war.

As the Allied armies advanced, many leading collaborationists, plus as many Milice as could escape, also fled to Sigmaringen. Finally, as the Allies punched deep into Germany, the Marshal's German guards drove Petain to the Swiss border and left him there on his birthday, April 24th, 1945. Petain made his way through Switzerland to France, where he gave himself up voluntarily to General Marie-Pierre Koenig.

The newly liberated French carried out a purge or "Epuration" of collaborators, ranging from the harrying of women suspected of engaging in sexual relations with Germans, to formal trials for many officials and Milice members. These courts handed out numerous prison terms and execution sentences, attempting to erase the blot of French collaboration with a round of rough, but legally correct, justice.

Pierre Laval paid for his avid collaboration with his life, sentenced to death and shot as so many Resistance members had been with far less cause and infinitely less care taken to assure a fair trial. Darnand, the head of the Milice, also met his death before a firing squad. Petain received a life sentence for treason, which he served out on the Ile d'Yeu, dying six years later in July 1951. At his trial, though he claimed that he acted only with "the knife at his throat," he offered his own life in exchange for that of any other men brought to trial for collaboration:

> my life matters little. I have given to France the gift of my person. It is at this supreme moment that my sacrifice must not be held in doubt. If you must condemn me, let my condemnation be the last, and let no more Frenchmen be condemned or imprisoned for having obeyed the orders of their legitimate leader (Griffiths, 2011, 254).

Overall, Vichy France represented an inevitability, given that Hitler wished to create a pliant rump state to assist with governing his largest western conquest. If Petain and Laval had not collaborated, someone else would have. They, however, chose to do so, and thus also accepted responsibility and blame for the evils visited on their country by the Germans during their occupation.

The authoritarian, conservative, and indeed reactionary government, culture, and society of Vichy France did not constitute an imposition by the alien conqueror. The Germans merely provided the conditions needed for a home-grown right-wing dictatorship to arise. Relatively mild at the beginning, the Vichy Regime grew steadily more repressive and violent as the war continued.

The failure of the Vichy economy – due in large measure, admittedly, to unreasonable Third Reich demands rather than failed policies – alienated the populace and necessitated either an end to collaboration, or progressively more naked terror to maintain control. Many Vichy leaders started as anti-Semites and found it quite easy to enforce Hitler's racial policies. Vichy attempted to build a strong France based on the values of a "new Middle Ages" and failed resoundingly in practically every way.

After the war, "liberty, equality, and fraternity" returned, despite the right-wing leanings of de Gaulle himself. The French economy rebounded, leading to thirty years of unprecedented prosperity despite the loss of France's overseas possessions; the famous French *joie de vrie* returned; and Paris, known during the war years as "The Extinguished City," became once more the City of Light.

Online Resources

Other World War II titles by Charles River Editors

Other titles about the Battle of Kursk on Amazon

Bibliography

Callil, Carmen. Bad Faith: A Forgotten History of Family, Fatherland and Vichy France. New York, 2006.

Christofferson, Michael, and Thomas Christofferson. France During World War II: From Defeat to Liberation. New York, 2006.

Corvaja, Santi and Robert L. Miller (translator). Hitler & Mussolini: The Secret Meetings. New York, 2008.

Grainger, John D. Traditional Enemies: Britain's War With Vichy France, 1940-1942. Barnsley, 2013.

Griffiths, Richard. Marshal Petain. London, 2011.

Hellman, John. The Knight-Monks of Vichy France: Uriage, 1940-45. Quebec City, 1993.

Horne, Sir Alistair. To Lose a Battle: France 1940. London, 2007.

Jackson, Julian. France: The Dark Years, 1940-1944. Oxford, 2001.

Passmore, Kevin. The Right in France from the Third Republic to Vichy. Oxford, 2013.

Pearson, Christopher. Scarred Landscapes: War and Nature in Vichy France. London, 2008.

Shirer, William. The Rise and Fall of the Third Reich: A History of Nazi Germany. New York,

2011.

Shlaim, Avi. "Prelude to Downfall: The British Offer of Union to France, June 1940." Journal of Contemporary History. Volume 9, No. 3, July 1974, pp. 27-63.

Smith, Colin. England's Last War Against France: Fighting Vichy 1940-1942. London, 2010.

Sumner, Ian and Francois Vauvillier. The French Army 1939-45 (I): The Army of 1930-40 & Vichy France. Oxford, 1998.

Sweets, John F. Choices in Vichy France: The French under Nazi Occupation. Oxford, 1994.

Manufactured by Amazon.ca
Bolton, ON

12834046R00026